The Art of CPA Affiliate Mastery:

The Proven Steps to becoming a Super Affiliate

I0481570

By Malik Johnson

Table of Contents

Introduction

Keene in New Hampshire is a quaint neighborhood that is popular for its pumpkin festival. High school sweethearts Andy and Matt who lived in this small place started making handmade toys as a hobby, while they were dating. Their friends loved their creations and bought them to gift each other for Secret Santa, besides other occasions. What started as fun and passion conveniently turned into a profession. Their small business grew through word of mouth and soon Matt opened a small factory (in his garage) and employed a few laborers to make the toys. Andy looked after the creative side of the business while Matt took care of finance and administration. They advertised through social media and started getting orders from all over the country. Matt realized that he'll have to expand the business, have more employees and start a bigger factory. He was looking for investments and that is when he found several investors online. After pitching to them he got funded and Andy and Matt were very happy about their business growth.

To make it financially viable they needed to advertise to a wider audience worldwide. That is when Andy came across Google's paid advertising campaign and decided to join the Google Adwords campaign. Andy and Matt also realized that they cannot market all by themselves. They needed to have a network of affiliates who will bring in the business. Matt moved their offline business online and got a payment gateway installed on their website. All the products were displayed on their e-commerce site and they offered holiday sales and discounts too. Thanks to affiliates their sales picked up speed. Matt and Andy were loaded with so much work that dealing with various affiliates became a task. Dealing with each one of them, checking their accounts to see how many leads and sales they've done and then paying them became an ordeal. Though the software did all the calculations Andy and Matt had to take a look at the data before making pay outs. That is when Matt heard about affiliate networks. They joined several CPA networks to find affiliates who could promote their product for a fee. They found hundreds of affiliates at Maxbounty and Peerfly, to name a few.

What are affiliate networks?

Affiliate networks are sites where all the affiliates gather and all the work of checking each affiliate is done by the network company. It is known as the CPA Super Affiliate. The major advantage of affiliate networks is you only have to deal with a single entity. Even if you've 50 affiliates selling your products; instead of dealing with each one of the fifty, you deal with this single network. They do the dirty work for you. Another benefit is you've the flexibility to join more than one affiliate network. Say you've joined three networks with each having 100 affiliates; that mean 300 affiliates are selling your product online. Every impression their page gets it helps your product to rank high on Google. The main difference between being an affiliate marketer and a CPA super affiliate is, as an affiliate marketer you only get paid a commission when there is a sale. As a CPA super affiliate you get paid for cost per action (CPA). Even if a person has just browsed or landed on the publisher's site from their mobile phone or computer; you as a super affiliate are paid.

Matt joined several super affiliate networks and had more than 500 affiliates pitching and selling his toys online. To his surprise every minute there was a sale and Matt and Andy became a millionaire couple, in a year's time thanks to CPA super affiliate networks.

Affiliate marketing has opened up a new area of marketing and sales for products all around the world. Today if you're not online means you're as good as dead. It is learnt that more than 2 billion users are on Facebook and Google mail. The market is wide open and anything and everything sells online. It's cheaper, easier and ROI (return on investment) is excellent. The beauty is it's free to be an affiliate marketer. So what are you waiting for? Go ahead read the ebook and get started! See the millions pouring into your account to lead the Big American Dream life.

Chapter 1 - What are affiliate programs?

Before we discuss about affiliate networks let's take a look at what an affiliate program is and how does it work? To put it simply affiliate program is where you sell somebody else's product for a commission. The advantage is you don't need to invest any money to be an affiliate marketer. All you need is zest and zeal to achieve and succeed online. The internet offers you affiliate marketing where in your website will earn you money even while you're sleeping as the process is automated. All you need is a sales page to promote somebody else's product.

It's not as easy as it seems. Well, nothing is easy when you've to make money. You need to invest your time and effort before you hear the jingle of money. There are several factors that need to be taken into consideration before you join an affiliate program. The first and foremost issue is – which product to promote? There are more than a million products online. How do you know which one to choose? It is here that you need to do due diligence.

You don't need any experience to become a super affiliate. You don't even need a college degree or proficiency in any field. As an affiliate you don't need to build your reputation. This is the hardest part in the sales process. Reputation building can take years and loads of money. As an affiliate you are ready to go. The hard work has been done for you.

People who have built their own online business know how difficult it is to create a payment gateway. Ask for the credit card details and the prospect will run away as if attacked by wild dogs. You don't have to be worried by the prospect of managing wild dogs. As an affiliate there aren't any. Managing a website, manufacturing a product, juggling the inventory and worrying about shipping and insurance are only a few issues which an affiliate does not have to bother about.

There are affiliate networks that bring together advertisers and affiliates to promote their products and sell. The affiliate network is a third party who links the publisher (affiliate) and a company to join affiliate programs. They offer a technical platform to recruit affiliates, manage and provide tools, tracking commissions and conversions, an instant access to a pool of affiliates and also identify frauds and tricksters.

An affiliate network acts like a bridge between publishers and manufacturers. Both gain thanks to these networks. The company can promote and sell their products on a platform where there are affiliate available and don't have to search for them. It's a single point access to many merchants who can instantly pick up their product. Some of these affiliate networks have more than 20,000 affiliates.

- As an affiliate joining a program is free. You just need to do your homework and pick products that you feel are good to be promoted.

- Make a website/ sales page to promote the product. Use all the content marketing tactics like keyword optimization and search engine friendly content, etc. Let your page look attractive and user friendly. Have testimonials of genuine people who have used the product.

- Link your site to that of the manufacturer. Remember that manufacturers are very particular about who promotes their product. You cannot fool them. Be genuine and sincere. Some even give you banner ads and book covers to put up on your site.

- Spend at least an hour every day trying to promote the product. Install Google analytics for your site and monitor the traffic. Alter content or design suitably to attract customers.

The affiliate network besides helping publishers and companies' link, also aggregates various offers from vendors, prepares a directory to find offers and handles all the administrative duties of the network.

How do they work?

Ten years ago affiliate marketing started as an Internet-based marketing practice in which you as a vendor reward one or more affiliates (website owning persons or companies) for each visitor referred to your website through their advertising and promotional efforts (affiliate's marketing efforts). Note, however, that you may also opt to become an affiliate for other vendors (some marketers prefer only to be affiliates promoting others products against commission, and do not have any product of their own). Affiliate marketing is somewhat akin to the system of compensation of sales personnel in traditional performance marketing where, typically, sales personnel are paid a commission for each sales they close (the CPA, CPC and the CPM models, however, do not require the affiliate to close the sale).

The affiliate marketing process involves four core players: the Merchant or Vendor; the network provider (e.g. Google for Google AdWords); the Publisher of Ads (the affiliate); and, of course, the Consumer. The affiliate marketing process essentially involves using other websites (affiliate websites) for advertising and promotion to drive traffic to your (vendor's) website; the affiliate being compensated in some way for his efforts.

The most common compensation methods in affiliate marketing are the 'Revenue Sharing' or 'Cost-Per-Sale (CPS)' model; the 'Cost-Per-Action (CPA)' model; the 'Cost-Per-Click (CPC)' model; and the 'Cost-Per-Mille (CPM)' model. In CPA (sometimes called Pay-Per-Action, PPA), the affiliate is paid by the vendor for each action (a purchase or form submission etc) linked to the Ad.; in CPC for every click; in CPM for every thousand views or impressions (Mille being thousand in Latin).

The popularity of the Cost-Per-Click system has diminished somewhat due to problems of 'Click Fraud' where unscrupulous marketers employ manpower or software to engage in repetitive clicks to earn more commission or to make it uneconomical for competitors. Many affiliate marketing network providers (Google, for instance) are taking active anti click-fraud measures to control the menace.)

Successful affiliate programs require constant monitoring and maintenance. This not only requires knowledge and experience, but is also very time consuming. Fortunately, expert outsourced affiliate program management (OPM) companies are now available to take the load off the internet marketer (affiliate or merchant, as the case may be). The main problem that remains in the sphere of affiliate marketing is the absence of any national or international regulatory authority to control undesirable activities like spamming, trade mark infringement, false advertising etc; or international standards of training or certification. A number of attempts have been made to create some sort of an industry body or association that could initiate action for developing ethical standards, guidelines and standards for the affiliate marketing industry, but without any success so far.

There are many affiliate programs which you can join. The process of joining an affiliate program is simple.

1. First you must have a look at what is on offer. There are many affiliate programs and therefore you must be able to identify one which gives you maximum returns.

2. Create a website to match the product you have chosen. Use all the tricks and advice provided in this book to create content which attracts buyers.

3. What have you learnt about creating an effective sales page? Make use of the strategies to promote the product you want.

4. Remember that you have already chosen the products which you want to sell. This is the time to join your chosen affiliate program. The advantage of beginning

with the end in mind is that your site is ready to be assessed. Many affiliate programs give you membership only after they have had a look at your website. Don't assume that you can fool them. Anyway, you won't make any money if you cannot attract buyers.

5. You can sign up for more than one affiliate program. You need to dedicate pages for specific products related to one affiliate program.

6. Don't sit back and wait for customers. You have to actively promote your site to attract good prospects.

7. Follow up with a good analytics program. Know what a visitor does on your website. Change content and design appropriately to increase your sales.

That's it. You are well on your way to becoming a Super Affiliate.

Types of affiliate programs

The most well known US CPS (click per sale) affiliate networks are

- Clickbank
- Commission Junction
- Amazon
- Linkshare
- ShareASale
- Avangate

These sites offer a commission only when you make a sale. The product link is embedded on your website or blog and when someone clicks on it they reach the affiliate site from where they buy the item. When a purchase is made, a commission is paid to the affiliate. This is the affiliate marketing strategy that was in vogue till now. The super affiliate network is slightly different from the original affiliate programs. In super affiliate the commission is paid as per CPA (cost per action). That means even if there is no sale if a person has even visited the product site, the affiliate is paid. The payment differs for each action. Be it CPA or CPS or PPC (pay per click) etc.

Clickbank works on this model. You can sell ebooks and digital products through Clickbank. They are pioneer in affiliate marketing and have a presence in more than 190 countries. There are almost six million clients worldwide and they're the within the top 100 successful companies online. Thanks to Clickbank there are several small business owners who have become millionaires. Clickbank assists in building visibility and revenue generating opportunities for entrepreneur's world wide.

Commission Junction also works in the affiliate marketing slot and offers commission to their affiliates for sale of goods and products. They've a wide range of products to choose from. You can choose more than one product and sell it to earn a commission.

Amazon also has its own affiliate program. You join the program (free) and get a link embedded on your blog/ page. Every click someone makes and reaches Amazon's site to buy, you get a commission.

It is actually not very easy to make money through affiliate programs. Whereas the CPA super affiliate program is one of the easiest ways to make money. You can easily make $300 per week just by recommending people from your blog/ page.

Linkshare, Shareasale and Avangate are all platforms where affiliates can make money. Before you join any affiliate program go through forums and their range of products to know exactly what you're getting into. There are many forums where super affiliates talk directly and guide you to make a buck online.

If you're already into affiliate marketing or trying to get into one, join a super affiliate program to earn super money online. Why put in effort that doesn't translate into money? Many people joined affiliate marketing on Clickbank and others and dropped out of it disappointed as they couldn't make a sale to earn a commission. After that they never went near an affiliate program.

Well, times have changed and super affiliate programs make you earn for a CPA (cost per action). So get started and put in some effort to become a super affiliate.

Chapter 2 - What is CPA?

CPA networks are websites where a publisher and a marketer can meet to promote a product. It is the intermediary between an advertiser and publisher. Cost per action (CPA) is the latest way to make money as an affiliate marketer. At one point of time only when a visitor made a purchase the affiliate was paid a commission. Whereas CPA affiliate marketer is paid for every action a visitor makes. Even if the person just browsed through the pages of the product you're promoting, you're paid an 'x' amount. Referrals are also paid a commission. From $1 to $100 depending upon the action the affiliate is paid a handsome amount. CPA affiliate networks are nothing but online advertising tools. The advantage of CPA affiliate is you earn more than an ordinary affiliate marketer.

Another advantage of being a CPA affiliate is you can market the products through mobile apps. This wasn't possible as an affiliate marketer.

Mobile performance marketing is when a visitor clicks to visit your product the publisher pays you CPM (cost per mille) i.e. 1000 impressions. This amount is paid regardless of the consequence of the click. That means even if the visitor has not made a purchase, still it is considered to be publicity.

Other actions that can earn money are filling a questionnaire, registering, subscribing to their newsletter, subscribing to SMS alert (mobile service) or any other action depending upon the affiliate program.

How does it work?

When a company wishes to promote their product and expand globally to generate at least 10,000 leads, a CPA network helps you to do just that. The network has various categories of programs and you can choose one of them to advertise your product. In case the network doesn't have the category for your product, they'll create one for you. The networks are genuine and work with you so that everyone involved stands to gain. Each product or program has statistics about how popular the product is and how much sales have taken place and earnings for the publisher, etc. It is updated real time so that you can choose which products to promote.

The EPC (earnings per click) shows how well the offer is converting and what is the payout per lead. To pick an offer the publisher can browse through the list of programs to see the best conversion campaigns/products/ programs. Look for the payout per lead to select your products. The publisher then clicks on the campaign name to receive the unique offer link that he can promote on his website or blog. Every visitor arriving at the offer page will be redirected to the CPA network system for the campaign offer.

As a publisher look for a campaign that offers low CPA and incrementally increase it. You can do a sample test to find out if the campaign suits you. This will help you to identify your customers. Also keep your mind open about the CPA network you join. You maybe a member at different networks where all the campaigns are running ; see to it that you offer the same rate at all the networks. Don't have price difference at different networks. It should be uniform.

As an advertiser your co-operation with the CPA network will help expand your customer base as well as sales. As a publisher you need to pick the campaigns that have high conversions as well as are popular and profitable. How to optimize your website/ blog, avail PPC, drive traffic to CPA network are all information you need to know to make money as a CPA affiliate. Keyword optimization is very important for a blog or website to arrive on organic search especially the first page. Gaining knowledge about search engine optimization will help in a big way to drive up the sales.

Advantages of CPA networks

You may wonder what the major benefit of joining a CPA network is. Here are some of the benefits –

- Your campaign gets global recognition
- Your technical issues are taken care of by the network
- Driving Traffic to your campaign
- It opens up new markets
- It's a cost effective marketing tool
- Makes business easier

As a CPA affiliate all you need to do is embed the campaign link (that is available in the CPA network) onto your website/blog. Technology takes care of everything else. Whenever there is a visitor visiting the CPA network the link automatically captures the behavior of the visitor and converts it into the action performed by the individual.

Networks also offer special tools to track real time conversion, banner and email tools, etc. They also offer readymade platforms for publishers and advertisers to meet, technical support, verified partners and campaign optimization. Each affiliate program can be a part of the CPA network.

LiveChat has introduced in-house affiliate programs. You get the best quality affiliate marketing materials that'll help you to improve in CPA field. You'll also be associated with high visibility brands that bring authenticity to your campaigns.

CPA networks are way better than Amazon affiliate network simply because the conversion rates are much higher than Amazon. If you're in the beauty business you can sell beauty products to get quicker and faster conversions. You can make around $300-$500 per week by promoting beauty products.

Types of CPA networks

There are more than 20 CPA networks available online. They're –

1. Maxbounty
2. Peerfly
3. Clickbooth
4. Neverblue
5. Matomy
6. W4
7. Adknowledge
8. Adscend Media
9. CPA way
10. Mundo Media
11. AboveAllOffers
12. Affiliate Venture Group
13. A4D
14. Convert2media
15. CPA trend
16. Fluent
17. Adperio
18. Adwork media

19. Millionaire Network
20. Diablo Media

Now let us take a look at how Maxbounty works –

Maxbounty is one of the most popular and top CPA network company that has the highest affiliates and advertisers with them. Having over 1500 active campaigns to promote on your website, Maxbounty is situated in Ottawa, Canada. For the past decade this CPA network is the number 1 in the affiliate industry. They've distinctly created a trust between affiliates and advertisers.

There have more than 20,000 affiliates who're ready to promote products that can earn high returns. Their affiliate number is growing and Maxbounty pays out more than a million dollars as affiliate commissions every year. Both the advertiser and affiliate has a lot to gain on this network. Maxbounty has more than 400 advertisers conducting several campaigns at the same time.

Maxbounty pays their affiliates for CPA (cost per action) i.e. just to fill up a form on their network or to sign in with email address and phone number or to give out credit card details; every action is paid for. Each offer has a payment range from $1 to $400. The low paying offers are the filling out forms whereas the higher conversions are for sale.

You can withdraw $100 at a time from their network. Having an account with Maxbounty as an affiliate you can link it to your PayPal or bank account so that once you get $100 you can transfer the funds to your account. Payoneer and Bitcoin are also accepted as mode of payments.

Be it a health product or make money online, every campaign is available on Maxbounty. Dating, relationship, clothing, fashion, Bitcoin and cryptocurrency are some of the popular campaigns running on this network. You can also start anew campaign if you don't find the particular subject you wish to pursue.

How to join Maxbounty?

It's simple and very easy to join this most popular CPA network.

Step 1- All you've to do is sign in for an account and wait for them to call you.

Step 2 - Their affiliate manager will have a telephonic conversation with you. She/ he'll ask you about why you wish to promote a particular campaign and what your awareness about the product, etc is. Once she's satisfied you'll be approved and allowed to log in.

Step 3 – Go through all the campaigns available and select the ones you wish to promote. You'll get an affiliate link for each campaign. Embed it on your website or blog.

There is a sign in bonus of $1000 if you make sales worth $1000 in the first 3 months. They also have a referral program where in you earn

5% of what the referral makes for a year. You can actually earn free money for someone else's work.

If you've a huge email list then you're the ideal candidate for becoming an affiliate on Maxbounty. Even a list of phone numbers will do as mobile marketing is also available.

Peerfly also is another popular CPA network that works on the line of Maxbounty. They're genuine and make regular payments. They've around 1900 campaigns running at the same time and there are more than 10,000 affiliates promoting them. They've a strong affiliate management team and respond immediately. Chad French is the founder and the network is competing in the CPA network area.

Besides CPA networks there are affiliate forums where the star affiliates who earn more than $100,000 per year share their views with others. You get to learn the tricks and secrets of these successful affiliates.

StackThatMoney Affiliate Forum – www.stm-forum.com is an affiliate forum that was started in 2011. The content is useful for newbie and already an affiliate. There is a membership fee of $99 to join this forum. This will be the only investment you'll make to know everything about affiliate marketing. There are more than 34,000 threads and 300,000 approx posts on this forum. The number is mindboggling and this forum is more like WIKI for affiliates.

There are more than five thousand members and at any given point at least 500 people are live on the forum. In case you've any doubts to clear or knowledge to gain, somebody is always there ready to help you. There are sections in the forum that cover important events and happenings in the affiliate industry. Weekly news updates on what happens at STM is also discussed there. Drew Whitmen, Charles Ngo and Dan Ariely are some of the super stars who're part of the forum. They clear your doubts and help you to get started as an affiliate marketer.

As a newbie you can join the forum to learn about how to choose a campaign to promote and also about how to get started as an affiliate marketer. There's an ONBOARDING ZONE that guides you step by step to make your journey as an affiliate marketer easy. There's also an information hub that'll advice you to follow the best practices to run your campaigns successfully. ANGLES are a section where tips for split testing are discussed in detail. Here you can learn how to present your campaign to the people. The words you use to grab attention and also the banner ads and landing pages are in display that has helped convert high ROI. You can simply cut and paste these onto your site/ blog.

There is a general section as well as a section on traffic. The traffic section is huge. You can look for tips on how to drive traffic using mobile, Google, Facebook, Native ads, Bing, Yahoo,

Adwords, YouTube, etc. The latest tips and updates are discussed here and 1 on 1 you can discuss about cheapest clicks and highest CTR (click through rate) to increase your profits.

In the general section you learn about tracking leads as this is the blood of affiliate marketing. Tracking your conversion will help you to focus more on the highest traffic puller tool so that you get more traffic from there. Also people share their story of how affiliate marketing has made them earn extra cash and how they've made their dreams come true. These stories are inspiring and give you hope to gain through affiliate marketing. STM success stories are motivating and they're real.

There is also a section where taxes are discussed. After all when you make $100,000 a year you need to be smart about them. STM also has an amazing section on health and lifestyle. Affiliate marketers are sitting in front of computer whole day. So they need to keep healthy by making lifestyle changes. Jogging, gymming, diets are all discussed here. There are also localized sections for every part of the world.

Chapter 3 – Get found on Google

How to do proper keyword research for your offers

Keywords are the main words that'll help the search bot to identify your website and rank you on the search. Identify words that are related to your niche and use them in the content you create on your website. In internet marketing content is king. Authentic and original content will drive traffic to your website; infuse keywords with it and you're sure to rank high on organic search. For example – if your business is about selling a weight loss product, look for keywords in that category. Create an account with Google and search for keywords and phrases in the weight loss niche. For example – fitness, weight reduction, lose weight, diet are some of the keywords used by all the weight loss websites. There are more than a million websites online on weight loss. Then how do you stay different yet be among the competitors? The keywords mentioned above are extremely competitive keywords. So you need to have key phrases and also identify secondary keywords that'll help you to stay ahead of competition.

'Weight loss' is a popular keyword, and a simple search may throw up 33,100,000 sites worldwide with material about it. Now that's a huge number and competition is indeed very high. Depending upon your product type you should look for alternative key phrases like weight loss for women or weight loss in diabetic men, teen weight loss and so on. This will throw up a substantially low search result like say 300,000 searches. Even this is quite high. Further refine your search and look for 'weight loss through holistic approach'. This phrase may have a far less search result of say 30,000 searches per month. Doesn't this make sense? Now, collect all these keywords and phrases to write articles. The keyword should ideally appear a maximum of 3% in your articles. You can use one each in every paragraph. A search using exact match will give you a more accurate picture of the potential traffic and competition.

Though you may feel that the long tail keyword of 'weight loss through holistic approach' is less competitive, remember you will be targeting the right audience. You may also insert the keyword phrase in your banner ads and your website url. That should do the trick. If you are targeting traffic to a specific area then you can add the area name to the keyword. Also get reviews written with keywords and post them in appropriate places. All these above mentioned methods will help to strengthen your campaign using Google keywords tool.

Pick keywords with the aim of generating adequate volume of qualified traffic; helping visitors in their buying-decision process; and finally, helping to convert prospects to customers. Generally, keywords selected should a judicious mix to take care of broad-match (usually single-word) and phrase-match or exact-match (usually keyword phrases) searches;

the former to generate traffic and the latter to filter and channelize quality traffic. Picking 'business-specific' or 'service-specific' keywords, when applicable, help facilitate the visitor's buying decision while 'power' or 'action' words, such as, say, 'buy now' used in keyword phrases can help conversions. 'Geographic' keywords can also be very useful for websites (and online businesses) catering to a localized or geographically delineated market. Online keyword research tools can greatly help to effectively pick keywords.

Look for secondary keywords and phrases at the keyword search tools page of Google. That'll throw up a whole lot of words and phrases. Check your competitor's website and see what all keywords they've used. Accordingly you can tailor make content to your web pages.

How do you identify a successful product?

Once you've selected the category, browse to see all the products posted there. The ones with high gravity are best sellers. Also the figures mentioned below the product shows how much commission an affiliate will get for promoting the product. The vendor spotlight will show you the history of the vendor and how many affiliates are promoting the product and also the website of the product. After doing a thorough research, 'click' on the 'promote' button. A 'hoplink' is generated that is your link for this specific product. Place the hoplink on your blog or landing page.

Landing page is a must

As an affiliate marketer it is important to have a landing page for each product with your specific hoplink. That will ensure that when a buyer clicks on your hoplink and reaches the product website to make a purchase, CB automatically sends the commission to you. The commission for affiliates on CB is as good as 60-75 %. That is a remarkable amount. For example, if you're promoting two products with an average commission of $50, selling 100 in number of the two products put together will earn you $5000 per month. Isn't that wonderful? A top affiliate on CB earns in millions. The trick is to promote more products to earn more.

Maximum expense for an affiliate will be to get a landing page done and get articles and newsletters submitted to market the product. That should not cost you more than $100. So you see it is very easy to make money as an affiliate. All you need is zest and zeal and some patience. It takes two to three months to get the first sale. After that there is no looking back.

Tracking tools

The most important aspect of any affiliate marketing program is to understand the behavior of clients. Google Analytics is specifically designed for this purpose. Google analytics is the best tool that can help you to give an idea about competitive keywords, number of organic searches, competitors in the field and where you rank among them. There are several tracking tools that can help you to known about your search engine ranking. They can identify keywords as well as check your back links, audit your web site and keep you updated about real time data. This is suitable for both IOS and Android apps. There are hundreds of tracking tools available now. We'll take a look at some of the most popular ones that are used extensively. Google analytics, Moz, SERP, Tracking Tarvis, SEO profiler, Authority Labs, Rank Watch, White Spark, AWR (advanced web ranking) Rank Scanner, Microsite Master and many more.

Before we look at other tools, let's take a look at -

Google analytics

You want to know who visited your site, how many, from where they arrived and how they behaved on it. Using this information you can change or refine your marketing strategy.

There are two ways by which data about the website traffic can be collected. You can collect data directly from your website or from the server on which your website is hosted. Technically, Google Analytics collects data from server logs. Much of the data residing on server logs is intelligible garbage. This mishmash of data is put in a readable format and presented to you by Google Analytics.

You can go deep into the performance of your website or affiliate page using Google Analytics. You can collect all sorts of web metrics which can eventually lead you to gather insight about the performance of your website.

The type of relevant metrics which you should measure and observe will enable you to understand the behavior of your visitors. You would be interested in knowing how people land on your website. This will throw light on which kind of advertisement is attracting customers. You can change your online marketing strategy to ensure better ROI or return on investment.

Essentially, Google Analytics will help you to gather information which will in turn provide insight. At first you will find it pretty difficult to understand this software, but over time it is likely to be your best friend. Don't give up on Google Analytics just because it seems difficult to grasp. There are hundreds of books out there which explain Google Analytics and how to use it. Suffice to say that it is one of the most important tools for any affiliate.

Google analytics uses a small code that is embedded in each and every page of your website. When traffic comes to your website the code gets automatically activated and starts collecting data on the behavior of the user who has visited your site. Google Analytics is the best tool to use as they've a huge presence on the web with enormous cloud infrastructure that will help you to make informed business decisions. It is FREE and very simple to use Google Analytics.

1. Sign in to your Analytics account.
2. Click Admin.
3. Select an account from the menu in the ACCOUNT column.

4. Select a property from the menu in the PROPERTY column.
5. Under PROPERTY, click Tracking Info > Tracking Code.

The tracking code is known as asynchronous tracking code that is more perceptive and perfect. This code can be placed between the HTML head tags so that when they're triggered they run parallel to page loading.

Split testing your campaign

How can you evaluate the effectiveness of your web copy? Is there a better way to attract customers? Does your headline grab the attention of the visitors? Can you improve on it? These are questions which can be effectively answered by A/B Testing or split testing.

The first step in split testing is to understand the dynamics of your website. By dynamics we mean the way various elements interact on your website. For example, you would like to know which one of the headlines is more effective. You can also compare different email content or a banner ad.

The process of split testing is simple. You must choose two version of the element you want to compare. In case of a website, you can have two different landing pages. You can direct fifty percent of visitors to each landing page. You can then observe the behavior of visitors and evaluate their effectiveness by comparing the conversion rates. Google Analytics can be used to measure conversion rates. This will enable you to choose the better landing page. You will no longer be working with assumptions and guesswork. You will have concrete figures and numbers to work with.

Generally split testing involves measuring or testing of two parameters. In case you have more than two options or variations to test you can chose two first, eliminate one of them and again test the better option with a third. Comparing more than two variables can give you confusing results.

Search Engine Optimization

SEO means optimizing your site for search engines. When you hit the search button after entering a word or phrase as a query, the search engine goes into overdrive. SEO is the art of getting your website noticed and ranked by major search engines so that it can be found by organic (natural) search enquiries.

You might have noticed that most of the times, whenever you use a search engine, the Wikipedia page always crops up. Why does this happen? Does Google have some understanding with the website owner? Some underhand ploy? You will agree that you will always find the right information on Wikipedia, whatever may be your search word or keyword. Can we say that Wikipedia site is relevant? Yes. What about other relevant sites? Your own site may be equally relevant but unfortunately Google does not agree with your opinion. The most important factor which Wikipedia has is authority. In essence

Wikipedia has both relevancy and authority. How do you position your website to be both relevant and authoritative?

Relevancy and Onsite SEO

Onsite means that which happens within your website. You must provide sufficient reason for Google to consider you as a relevant website. The first step in this direction is to have appropriate content on your website. Google, for that matter any search engine, is not human. It's an algorithm which tries to imitate human intelligence. It cannot differentiate between a scientific paper and a homemade recipe. But it has a great memory. It finds the keywords associated with your web page and stores this information including the number of times it appears on the web page in its memory. There was a time when SEO experts simply loaded a web page with keywords. For example, the keyword 'clothes' would be repeated a hundred times on a web page making it most relevant. Google saw through the sham and introduced something called keyword density. If a keyword exceeded a certain number in the page, then it is red flagged by the Google search engine.

Keyword density became an important part of onsite SEO. As of today 2 to 3% keyword density seems to be acceptable to Google. Onsite SEO also takes into consideration how the content is structured. The page title and sub headings and many other parameters are factored into the Google algorithm to decide relevancy of your web page.

Now, there may be hundreds of web pages which may be equally relevant. Keyword density alone cannot be the sole criteria to judge which pages should appear in SERPs (Search Engine Results Page).

Note: Why is Google picky about the whole process? Why not dump search results into the SERP? This is a good question which bothers many people, especially those who are new to SEO. The answer is really very simple. Imagine that you search for 'clothes' and you get results which have a vague connection with 'clothes'. If this happens continuously, you will stop using Google search. What's the point you will ask? Google will no longer be a popular search engine. Within a year, Google will end up broke and may have to shut its operations. Now you know why Google tries its hardest to show the most relevant results – their life depends on it. When it's a question of life and death, you better be careful. Google has therefore found other ways to identify the best websites which are relevant to search keywords.

Off page SEO

Have you heard about 'Link building'? A major part of SEO consists of 'Link building'. By creating links to your website you are signaling the Google search algorithm that your site is important – other websites want to be associated with you. As a result you become an authority. Therefore you must have inbound links to satisfy Google search algorithm that you deserve or merit a mention on the first page of SERPs. It's easy to imagine that SEO guys found a way to shortcut the link philosophy. Thousands of link farms sprouted up on the internet promising instant link nirvana. You simply had to pay a few bucks and the smart guys would provide a hundred back links in no time. There are hundreds of guys out there trying to game the system. Big websites pay millions to SEO professionals just to enter the legion of first page SERPs. There is always the danger of getting blacklisted by Google for trying to game their algorithm. This can also happen to you and getting out of the blacklist can be tough. So, don't try to game the system. Here you will learn legitimate ways to master SEO.

As you can very well guess, Google put an end to the link farm fiasco. They modified their algorithm to only include links which came from legit sites. All the link farms disappeared overnight. Google can be ruthless sometimes.

Link building is an important part of offline SEO. Can you get a link from Wikipedia? Your website will jump the queue and land on the first page of SERPs if you can manage a link here. It's clear that you have to link to sites which have authority. There are many ay to do this besides Wikipedia.

Link building is a tedious process. Every link matters and you must be careful who you choose to link with. Some SEO experts will suggest that you get reciprocal links from authoritative sites. Google has factored this into their algorithm and the new is that you will get not more than a drop of link juice from this arrangement. You will learn more about link juice later in this book.

Why not get links from other blogs? You can launch a hundred one page blogs and put a link in each one of them. The problem with this approach is that blogs are not considered as authority sites (except a few popular blogs). You will be wasting your time and effort if you try to fool Google.

SEO is a pretty simple process but there are no shortcuts. Use white hat tactics and get yourself found on organic search. That'll help you to sell your product online.

Pay-Per-Click (PPC) advertising

There are two components of internet or online search marketing. They're Search Engine Optimization (SEO) and Pay-Per-Click (PPC) advertising. While shopping online, a visitor may (or may not!) click on your Ad which appears on the search engine results page or a web page (also termed a 'Landing page') which he has reached (or 'landed' on) by keying in his search keyword or phrase. Pay-Per-Click (PPC) works on the principle that you (the advertiser) pay a predetermined price (or bid amount) to the search engine provider *only* when a visitor clicks on your Ad. PPC traffic can be accessed (purchased) from specialized PPC search engine operators. There are, literally, hundreds of such providers available on the net, but it's advisable (and safer) to choose one of the leading (though somewhat costlier) sponsors such as, for instance, Google, Yahoo! or MSN.

The use of PPC has become very popular with both merchants and affiliates (who promote products and services of others i.e. of merchants/ vendors) as a promotional tool in internet marketing. PPC search engine marketing is aimed at driving targeted traffic (potential buyers) to a website promptly and efficiently; and provides speed, flexibility and economy not only to vendors, affiliates and website sponsors, but also to consumers. One of the greatest advantages of PPC is that, unlike other types of advertising and marketing, the Ad is presented directly to the target market. This greatly increases the chances of a better return on investment as compared to other more conventional advertising modes.

Using PPC does not mean that the traditional 'marketing mix' should be overlooked (as many businesses unfortunately tend to do). In fact, the 4p's of marketing (product, place, price and promotion) are as important in internet marketing and PPC advertising as any other marketing strategies; particularly in the present economic environment. The *product* (or service) being offered should be saleable and should be such that *promotion* through search engine marketing (SEM) is possible. The website should be 'optimized' so that the *place* at which the Ad is displayed on the search results page is high enough (based on a combination of factors beyond the scope of this discussion) to attract attention but still economical (the click-price rises for higher displays). And, of course, the *price* point should be compatible with the product, place and promotion (and competition!)

Using PPC also does not mean that you abandon all other traditional marketing strategies. PPC may be a very important instrument in building up your business, but it certainly is not the only one; it should be just one implement in your marketing tool box! While PPC advertising has many advantages (it efficiently directs quality traffic – people who are already searching for your product category - to your website), it can very easily become uneconomical (as competition for your keywords increases, with consequent increase in click rates). Sometimes, your product may be such that while PPC advertising works, more traditional marketing strategies may work better and be more profitable.

Hence, your advertising and marketing strategies should always be a judicious mix of the traditional methods and PPC advertising, where PPC is just one component (albeit a very important one!) of your marketing arsenal.

Scaling up your sales

Whatever you may be doing about SEO and link buildings, remember that you need to drive up your sales. Each and every step you take should be towards that. This is known as conversion optimization. Your leads should get converted into sales.

Here are some tips that can help you to scale up your sales.

1. Make your product attractive with great design and eye catching colors.
2. Get email marketing done on a regular basis. Add new email addresses to your existing list.
3. Have 'form submission' on your website. When a visitor visits your site have a pop up form where in the visitor leaves his email address. That'll help you to identify prospective customers. You can later correspond with them to get a feedback about their experience on your site.

4. As a super affiliate marketer you get paid for a lead/ visitor as well. If that visitor buys then your commission goes up. Using analytics check how many leads you got and divide it by the buyers who purchased to arrive at the conversion rate.

5. Besides 'add to cart' and 'buy now' have a 'buy later' button on your page. You can get in touch with the visitor who clicked on it (buy later), to know what made them stop from buying. Depending upon the response, devise innovative methods to lure them.

6. Make your headlines bold and clear. The visitor should be able to get attracted by it.

7. Keep site navigation smooth. Remove navigation bar from landing pages. Keep your visitor focused on the product and encourage him/ her to buy. If there is a navigation bar then the buyer may deflect and move away from buying the product to look at other products.

8. Keep the text near the call to action (CTA) optimized. This can considerably increase conversion rates.

9. Don't stuff your landing page with excess information. Let there be some white space on the page. Highlight only about your product and its advantages. There should be breathing room for your website.

10. Make font size larger, so that it is easy to read. Don't use flowery language. Keep it simple and to the point. That is what will endear visitors to your product.

11. Avoid using stock photos. Use real photos of your product and people who have used them. Having genuine pictures gives authenticity to the product. You can also have reviews, awards if any, case studies, testimonials that can help people make informed decisions on your site.

12. Have your website/ landing page secured with validation. VeriSign secured sites are preferred. Google, PayPal, Norton are all

prominent and well known brands that people trust. Having industry specific seals will enhance your product's genuinity.

13. Money back guarantee and return policy will help the customer to buy the product. He knows that he can always return if it's not satisfactory.

Email Marketing

Email marketing includes marketing to opt-in lists, newsletter marketing, and marketing via bulk emails. Of the three, bulk email marketing tends to be the most unsuccessful as most people delete these hard selling mails from their inbox without even sparing them a read. After all, given the number of bulk emails we get, there are few other options. However, opt-in lists and newsletters offer good scope for organizations seeking to promote their business. This is because potential customers choose to get these emails because they are interested in what a company has to offer.

When one has acquired an interested potential customer base, holding that base becomes very important. The trick to holding on to that customer through email marketing is to show him that you care. You need to build up a relationship with him and make him look forward to your emails. Let him develop a certain trust for you before you start hard selling your product.

Building that relationship with your subscriber may not be easy, but it is not rocket science. Here are a few tips that you could follow when starting your email marketing campaign:

- Create a subject line that holds the attention of your subscriber.

- Offer valuable new information in every email. Do not just dish out the same old jargon. Provide tips and tricks that will keep your subscriber thirsting for more.

- Remember that this is a business letter. Personalize it but maintain a degree of formality. Remember that you are not on back-slapping terms with your subscribers.

- Encourage feedback.

There are several other aspects that could ensure that your email marketing campaign yields results. Find out what works for you.

Finally your product should be good enough for people to want it. Make it appealing and scale up your sales to hear the jingle of money. As a super affiliate your income should be able to help you buy that condo you so wished to buy. Start saving your super affiliate income and let all your dreams come true.

Chapter 4 – Convert traffic into customers

We have seen that the attention span of people surfing on the net is phenomenally short and the first impression that your website makes on the visitor is all important. The importance of keeping your website up-to-date with the latest information and content cannot be over stressed; it will determine what type of image you present. Outdated information or information that repeat visitors have seen over and over will likely make them quickly steer away from your site.

On the other hand, fresh and relevant information on your website is a compelling reason for visitors not only to visit your site but also to return to it if they know that they will see something new the next time they visit. They are also likely to bookmark your site and recommend it to others. Keeping your website always updated is, therefore, an excellent (in fact, essential) marketing strategy. Unfortunately, however, many website owners and webmasters are so busy running their companies or marketing campaigns that updating or refreshing their sites does not feature in their list of priorities; an omission that often, unknowing to them, has serious adverse effects on their businesses.

Content that you can conveniently change and update are articles and features on topics relevant to your product or service category, technical papers (if applicable), as well as interactive elements. Informative articles, interesting features and interactive elements are all hallmarks of a good website, but you cannot afford to just put them in place on your website and sit back and wait for tons of traffic to roll in. You *must* change the articles and features frequently, add new things, rotate old items and even change (update) the appearance of your web pages from time to time. Another way to quickly and simply keep content on your website fresh is to add a blog; the entries you post (preferably on a regular basis) and comments posted by users automatically contribute in keeping the site updated.

An interesting and useful spin-off from keeping your website updated to attract new and repeat visitors is the fact that in addition to increased loyalty and repeat traffic, updated websites tend to achieve higher rankings in search results. This may be due to most search engine algorithms probably working on the logic that updated websites have more to offer in terms of new, valuable content which web surfers look for.

There are a few actions that you, as the website owner or webmaster, need to take to be able to undertake the updating of your website effectively. Firstly, you have to stay updated on what is happening in the search engine industry; one way of doing this is to read blogs, newsletters, forum postings, white papers and case studies etc. As mentioned in the very introduction to this book, knowledge is the one most powerful tool that you will have for success of your internet marketing venture. Secondly, continuous testing and review of your website (its performance, content and looks) will help you to decide how to keep it fresh and interesting. Thirdly, it helps to have a plan and schedule for updating various website elements systematically.

The primary goal of your website is to convert visitors to customers. Even if you are able to generate high traffic, your online marketing efforts will be wasted if you are not able to convert visitors to leads (interested people who fill out a form, e-mail you or telephone you etc); and leads to customers. The majority of quality leads come from natural search, networking efforts and paid (say, PPC) advertising; with smaller streams usually from e-mail marketing, direct telemarketing etc. You must have a well designed plan to deal with the different categories of leads for optimum conversions; otherwise much of your efforts will be wasted. In other words you have not only to generate leads;

you have to nurture the leads till the buying decision is taken.

A well conceived plan for dealing with leads should basically have components which deal with questions such as: (a) which leads out of your total database of leads are you going to nurture? (b) What information are you going to provide the target groups or selected leads? (c) How are you going to communicate with the different groups selected? (d) How will 'leads' be assisted to transit from your lead nurturing program to actually taking action? Selecting the 'Leads' for your nurturing program has to be done carefully. You cannot obviously nurture every lead on your database; neither can you have a one-size-fits-all program for all. Firstly, identify the types of leads (existing customers, new leads, leads not yet ready to buy, trial customers etc) you want to target and their numbers and prioritize. Secondly, develop 'offerings' (brainstorming is a good way for this) that are tailored to persuade each group to take the action they are expected to take. Thirdly, after you have finalized the "offerings', is to decide how you are going to communicate with each selected group (same mode of communication for all groups is not likely to be effective). Communication options may range from the basic 'auto-responder' to sophisticated multiple-messaging systems; your choice will depend upon the audience/ segment you are nurturing. Finally, you have to design the exit destination of the nurturing program; direct the 'Lead' to action (buy now) through a special 'offer' or to a second nurturing program (for new leads not ready to buy yet) and so on.

While a detailed nurturing program such as the one outlined, is essential to effectively deal with leads, you need to keep two important aspects in mind. The first is that the success of a lead nurturing program depends on the 'quality' of leads. Ensure that you have quality leads; avoid buying ready-made lists of 'leads' from dubious companies on the Internet. Secondly, remember that success in online marketing also depends on the trust you are able to build up in the minds of customers and prospects. Always ensure that you follow best practices and regulations for the protection of customers and their personal data. This pays off handsomely in the long run.

Native Ads

Once you have optimized your website and submitted it to various search engines and online directories. To get it listed for organic searches you have to consider additional ways of promoting your site. Remember that simply building a site and submitting it to search engines and online directories for free promotion does not guarantee an instant audience. The additional avenues that you have for promoting your website and for driving more traffic to it are various types of paid advertising options. Ideally, you should employ a combination of free and paid forms of online advertising. Including a combination of free and paid advertising in your overall online promotion strategy can often mean the difference between the success and failure of your internet marketing program.

Internet marketing covers a wide range of marketing and promotional techniques and enables the use of various online marketing tools which includes paid advertising. Paid advertising itself has many forms including Banner Ads, Classified Ads, advertising in online magazines, local online directories, as well as online newsletters etc. The other form of paid advertising (and one of the most important) is 'Pay-Per-Click' (PPC) advertising which has not been discussed in detail in chapter 3. Let us understand here why we need to resort to paid advertising and expend scarce advertising budget when we can get free website promotion through search engine optimization and organic listings.

The need for paid advertising, subject of course to availability of budget, stems from certain shortcomings (difficulties would be a more apt word) inherent with organic or search engine marketing. The first problem with organic search marketing is that you need to ensure that your website gets listed within the first two (or at the most the first three) search engine results pages; internet users are an impatient lot and most internet users will not go beyond the first two or three pages of the search results displayed against their search terms (if they do not find what they are looking for, they would normally change their search term – use a variation – and try again). As all website owners would be trying to get listed at the top of the first page, getting onto the first two or three pages is a difficult, time consuming and continuing task, needing considerable research and experimentation to optimize your website and get all elements 'just right'.

The second problem (or difficulty, as we have mentioned) is that search engine optimization (SEO) is easier said than done; it takes a lot of knowledge, experience, effort and time (more than many internet marketers can, or are willing to, expend) to do all that is necessary to get such high rankings. A third problem is that it takes considerable time (sometimes even months) for search engines to index and list your website; and every day's delay means that you lose the opportunity for sales conversion.

On the other hand, pay-per-click advertising enables your website to be listed on search results pages within a few days (sometimes a few hours or even minutes!) after you open a PPC account with one of the pay-per-click search engine providers (Google, Yahoo! and MSN are some of the major providers in this field). If you have the budget, you can arrange to have your PPC Ad listed at the very top of the search engine results page (though that's not a cost-effective strategy as we shall presently see). Further, even though a lot of experimentation and effort is required to select keywords for higher listings (as in organic search engine optimization), even beginners can quickly learn the ropes to get started.

Considering all aspects, it is always advisable as mentioned at the outset, to adopt a combination of organic search marketing and paid advertisement in your website promotion strategy. Within the range of paid advertising tools available, pay-per-click advertising should definitely be considered even in a small way, to start with, if budget is a constraint. Effective paid advertising in any form is a valuable support for your online marketing efforts.

Chapter 5 - Advertising platforms

Now that you've selected campaigns to promote and have optimized your landing pages/ website/ blog you need to promote them. This is the litmus test as marketing your products is all about conversions. How you project your products and the powerful content you write on your site will decide the fate of your campaigns. It is here that you need to advertise through social media. Social media engagements are not a one day affair. You need dedication and staying power- something like having a serious love affair. You have to build relationships over a period of time. There are no quickies. There is a mistaken belief that once you have a Facebook account you can lie down and relax. Unfortunately, things don't happen that way. Social media campaigns have to be sustained over a long period of time. The term used here is 'engagement'. How to keep your customers interested? This is the first question which should pop up in your mind. You have to fall back to traditional marketing techniques. Keeping your customers happy is an art which works even today. Remember the 4 P's – Price, Product, Promotion and Place. You might have firsthand experience of participating in online shopping. What do you remember about it? Pricing always wins. Your product, of course, must speak for itself. The best part about social media is the word-of-mouth marketing. Word spreads like wildfire when you offer something attractive. This is also called viral marketing – when your customers become your best salespeople.

Coming back to the relationship issue, it takes time and considerable effort to make your presence felt on social media. You have to be at it constantly. Once your presence is acknowledged, your audience will experience a cascading effect. Friends of friends of friends will recommend your product and you will start attracting customers out of the blue. Don't expect this to happen within a day or week or even a month.

Maturation takes much longer and a year seems like a good target.

Relationships are built brick by brick. It takes time to build a reputation online but a single bad review can bring down your house in an instant. You should have a strategy to counter negative review. Offering immediate refund without asking questions can lead to redemption. Beware of your competitors trying to malign you by planting bad reviews. Social media marketing can be vicious and often is. Don't think it's a lovey-dovey place where love flows uninterrupted. On the other hand you don't have to do anything new. You don't have to discover new strategies. Simply look at your successful competitor and create a template. It's a very simple and effective strategy. Social media marketing can turn out to be simple if you are smart.

You must also engage your audience seamlessly over many social media platforms. If you want to announce a discount you may look at Twitter. At the same time, you may like to engage your customers on Facebook, though you may not get an instant response. Events like clearance and flash sales are occasions to drum up sales. Here time is of essence. In such situations, an email newsletter may not work as well as Twitter. Long term social media engagements must be punctuated by small tactical bursts of tweets. This will allow you to maintain the excitement and freshness of your marketing campaign. Let your customers anticipate the next tweet while you feed them with regular news through other platforms.

Understanding social media

Using social media like Facebook for fun and using it for business are two different things. You should not be afraid of making mistakes, but having said that, your marketing campaign can flounder for months if you don't know how the ecosystem works. You should not assume that you know all about Facebook, just because you are using it. Of course, you will start off well if your awareness level is good. To excel in social media marketing you must go into the details of each platform. Twitter is a totally different ball game compared to Instagram. Both are effective platforms for marketing but have different approach. Therefore, you should not be afraid to get your feet dirty in the social pond. In fact, more you learn, more you will be able to come up with winning strategies. Don't think that social media is easy. It's easy but only when you have in-depth knowledge.

These are some of the popular social media platforms –

Google +

YouTube

Bing

Facebook

Instagram

Twitter

LinkedIn

Pinterest

Google +

Google + is an amazing social media platform that connects you with likeminded people. You just need to key in the right words and your profile is likely to get friends from your fraternity. The advantage of Google + is your email is linked and so is your search page. Google+ takes all this into account and throws up the right audience for you. Though it is not all that popular like Facebook it has its own niche audience. Google + boasts that they've 250 million users and out of them 50% log in everyday. When you're promoting your business it is better to be seen and heard on all social media platforms.

Include keywords and relevant links on your About page. This will explain your business to your audience. You can link back to specific pages on your website from your About page. Make sure that your website pages are SEO friendly. Get Authorship. It's the best way to get your picture next to your listings in search results. Google authenticates you through Authorship and will begin to trust you as quality source of content. It is very simple to get Authorship. This will throw up your profile on search results resulting in higher ranking and click through rates.

YouTube

Video marketing is caught on like wild fire and YouTube is raking in the profits. Your videos go viral and people like to watch your product visually. If you're selling beauty products you can put up videos on how your make up tutorials transform a woman into a beauty. Looking at a 'normal' girl turn into a Diva immediately helps in conversion. Everyone likes to look beautiful and that is why make up tutorials are a big hit on YouTube. Your product should be appealing to customers and that is when you'll see traffic visiting your site.

There are more than 1 trillion videos on YouTube. Every second 5 hours of videos are getting uploaded. The number is appalling and staggering. Video marketing is the future and that is where the world is moving.

In your video explain about your product and have a call to action page from where the visitor clicks to enter your website. Also encourage visitors to opt in. Also they can subscribe and like your videos. This will help you to gain email addresses with which you can later approach them through email marketing.

Reviews are another great way to convince customers that your product is genuine. As an affiliate you can encourage visitors to listen to reviews of this product and then encourage them to buy from your link. This will help to a large extent.

You can also have training videos where you can help visitors how to use the product. Then you embed a link at the end of the video so that people reach your landing page to buy.

Timing is very important here. Your video shouldn't be more than 3 minutes. Else viewers will get bored and move away. Make it eye grabbing and keep the viewer glued to the screen.

Bing

Bing search belongs to Microsoft and is popular among Internet Explorer users. Though they give all details about shopping, travelling and other search queries Bing isn't as popular as Google search. As an affiliate marketer if you wish to place an advertisement on Bing it'll be placed in Yahoo search too as both have a partnership. Your ad will receive widespread visibility driving traffic to your landing page.

The reviews given by Bing on products selling on Amazon helps customers to buy with much ease. They don't have to look further than Bing search as they provide the best and authentic reviews. Shoppers find it easy to use Bing than Goggle for this.

Though Google is the Dinosaur that holds 65% of search market share, Bing and Yahoo put together hold around 9% and 21% respectively. Yet Bing does attract traffic from travel, health related searches.

Advertising on Bing is cheaper than Google. There are also free ads available. Open an account, find keywords, create your campaign, enter keyword and choose match types and write your ad. You can even import your Google Adwords. It's very simple and easy to use. As an affiliate you don't know from where you can get customers.

Facebook

Nowadays everybody, when I say everybody it means the entire world is on Facebook. Whether you're living in a tiny town in Zimbabwe or a village in the Amazon region, everybody is out there on Facebook. When you make an advert, Facebook asks you to target the age group of the audience, their place of stay and sex. Accordingly they look for similarity between the advertisement and the public's profile to place the ads on the right side of those profiles. Facebook analyzes your profile to see your feeds, the pages you and your friends like as well as your profile. They share your phone number and email address with the business and they add it to their customer list. They also connect through your IP address, your location through GPS and setting up of your Facebook and Instagram profile.

Once the ad starts to appear on the right side of the profiles you only pay if someone 'clicks' on them and reaches your page. There are two aspects to your billing methods. Budget and spend. Budget is the amount you set aside for the ad and the spend is how much you've actually spent. For example – say you've a budget of $100 but only $60 is spent because the clicks were only for that amount then your budget is $100 whereas your spend is $60. There is also a daily budget and lifetime budget for the ads.

There are more than 2 billion people on Facebook. The numbers are mind boggling. Take advantage of Facebook advertising and sell your products there. See the traffic reaching your landing page and the conversion rate is sure to be faster than other social media platforms.

Instagram

Instagram is the latest fad and it is here to stay. Everybody is on Instagram selling their products. There are more than 500 million users and the number is increasing by the day. In USA youngsters have stopped suing Facebook and have turned to Instagram. The ease of use is the reason for this. Your message instantly reaches your followers. Kim Kardashian, the celebrity advertised her makeup products and made it a global name with just one post. That is the power of Instagram. One post and your product reaches millions of users. The trick to add followers on Instagram is you follow your friends, their friends and their friends. For example you sent follow request to 1000 people and out of them at least 100 would follow you back. This way you build up your list of followers. Once you've more than 500 followers, promote your product on your page. At least 10% will visit your landing page and 1% will buy your product. This is a modest estimate. Increase your followers to

10,000 and the number of conversions will automatically increase. It's free to promote on Instagram. As an affiliate marketer you should take advantage of this free marketing tool to make money.

Twitter

It is an online application which helps people communicates with each other using maximum of 140 characters. When a person communicates or tweets, the message is instantaneously sent to many thousands of followers. There can be no better tool than Twitter to amass a fan following in your niche. Remember that the world is your audience here. You can reach the tip of Iceland and the jungles of Amazon with Twitter-that too instantaneously. You can actually populate your niche with Twitter followers. Because you have a passion for your particular niche, the enthusiasm and energy would automatically get passed on through your message. The response would also be equally enthusiastic, leading to a viral loop.

US President Donald Trump uses Twitter to reach out to people. So does many other heads of States and country. Such is the power of social media. There are more than a Billion users on Twitter. It's a world of its own. Use advantage of this amazing media to promote your affiliate marketing endeavors. Nowadays Twitter also allows images and videos to be posted on your accounts.

Chapter 6 - How to become a super affiliate?

- Find your niche

All of us are passionate about something or the other. While some like sports others like arts. You may be a fitness freak or a diehard pet lover. If you're none of these then at least you're worried about your health? Or interested in dating and sex? Well, you've to have some interest, right? Find your niche and choose programs in them to promote.

- Be creative

Have a unique signature for your landing pages. Create a style that is only yours and make yourself look different from others. Be creative and sky is the limit for you to make money through affiliate marketing.

- Be aggressive

Never do anything half hearted. Put your heart and soul into your programs. Be aggressive about your marketing gimmicks. Don't leave any stone unturned.

- Prioritize financial goals

Before you spend on your campaigns make a budget. Prioritize your goals as to how much you will spend for what part of the campaign. Once you're clear about these things start your campaign. Always keep your finances under check.

- Reach out to customers and retain them

Retaining customers is the best part of marketing. When there is a purchase talk to your customer for feedback. If there's anything negative ask them for reasons. Try and resolve their problems. Don't hesitate to refund your unsatisfied customers. That'll help build your reputation.

- Believe in yourself

Finally be confident and believe in yourself. If you don't believe then how will your customers have faith in you? Stay positive and be optimistic.

Chapter 7 - Case studies

Case Study 1

Charles NGO is one of the top super affiliate marketers online. Though he earns a seven figure income a year his secret sauce for selecting campaigns is not revealed to you. He talks about having landing pages, banner ads and creating a list for advertising through mobile phones, etc. The secret to his success is he chooses his products according to market needs. He promotes more than 10 products at a time and promotes them through Facebook and mobile marketing. According to Charles paid advertising through Facebook is the best way to promote products. There are many super affiliates like CharlesNgo who make a million dollar easily by joining CPA networks.

Charles Ngo is an Asian who is in the affiliate marketing industry for the last 10 years. He's known as the thought leader of the industry and he has more than 75,000+ followers who read his blog posts and respond to his tweets. He's a millionaire at the age of 30. He made his first million through affiliate marketing in the very first year he started. Since online marketing was at its infancy Charles had purchased something from a store that he sold on Ebay and made a profit. He found it interesting and did that for a while till Ebay black listed him. Since he already tasted success he joined affiliate sites to promote products. He started his own website and blog and promoted the products. Using social media and various other Google tools he promoted his products. For every sale he made he received a commission and Charles started talking about his success stories to people online.

He put up his monthly earning statements for everyone to see. From earning $500 per day he became a super affiliate by earning $30,000 per month. Even when Google changed its search parameters and websites took a beating, Charles income was steady at $1500/ per day as he was using proven techniques to drive traffic to his site. He joined CPA networks not only as an affiliate but also as a vendor. He promoted as well as sold his own products. He changed the products he promoted from time to time as per public requirements. He started to make $200,000 approx per month. This innovative experiment catapulted him into the millionaire category.

The main secret Charles talks about is mobile marketing. In CPA mobile marketing helps you to earn a handsome amount. For example- You enter a person's phone number and he gets a text message. When that person enters the pin, you get paid. The advertiser makes money by billing them $10 a month in their plan.

When you post an ad and a person clicks on it, he's taken to the app store. If he installs the app, you get paid.

You want a moving service to shift your home. You go on Google search from your phone and look for a moving service nearby. The affiliate marketer has subscribed for Pay Per Call on Google search. When you click on the number the call gets connected and the affiliate marketer gets paid.

Battery saving apps, Anti-virus and performance boosters are popular apps that can earn money for an affiliate on mobile.

Here are some mobile affiliate networks that you can use-

- YepAds
- Avazu
- Mobidea
- ClickDealer

You can buy mobile traffic from many places.

Case Study 2

Here's the story of Luba Goodman who became an affiliate marketer on Clickbank in the year 2007. She was a high school pass out and was a stay at home mom. Not having any skills she didn't know what products to choose. She did a simple research on Google and realized that people look for health products and pet food online. She joined around 10 affiliate programs on Clickbank.com and created landing pages for each one of them. She started with pregnancymiracle.com, ovariancystnomore.com, yeastinfectnomore.com, acidrefluxnomore.com, dietsolutionsprogram.com and a few more health related campaigns/ programs. She started a blog and wrote about her experiences as to how she got pregnant after 8 years of marriage thanks to pregnancymiracle.com that is a holistic healing method to get pregnant and have a safe delivery. Her genuine story attracted visitors and she could sell more than 600 of them in a year's time at $39.99 per piece. She became so busy that she had to employ a couple of people to run her affiliate programs. She constantly got articles written from ghostwriters and published them on online article directories to get back links. She automated the process and regularly updated her blog, put up testimonials on her landing pages, SE optimized her pages and published articles on ezine.com and several other directories. Her page rank improved and she appeared on the first page of Google search for the keywords – get pregnant, yeast infection, ovarian cyst, acid reflux and holistic treatment.

In two years time all her 10 products were getting her enough money to go on a world tour. But as luck would have it Google changed its search algorithm in 2011 and bang!! Her page rank fell and all the landing pages were unrecognized by Google. They blacklisted the landing pages. By then social media was gaining prominence and Facebook became the best place to promote products. Luba jumped on to Facebook and had pages about her campaigns there. She also joined forums to attract visitors to her site.

Luba also realized that she needed more products to promote and looked outside the health arena. She picked pet food and products that would sell well. Dog food, pet grooming were hot topics at that time and Luba picked pet related campaigns. She also promoted relationship programs like secretstoalastingmarriage, howtostaymarried, etc. This time around she moved to social media, had pages for each of the products, joined forums, invited people to visit her sites. She also wrote an ebook on being a successful affiliate marketer. This brought in visitors from all over the world and Luba made a million dollar just talking about her success as an affiliate marketer. She travelled around the world sharing her experiences about being an affiliate marketer.

Around 2013 she posted videos on YouTube and Podcasts about her success in the online arena. She became a super affiliate thanks to MaxBounty.com, Peerfly.com, and neverblue.com from where she received traffic to her campaigns. Her income multiplied and after 4 years Luba has more than a million visitors coming to her sites and the ROI (return on investment) is terrific. She's a super affiliate who makes $200,000 a year thanks to CPA affiliate mastery.

Case Study 3

Pat Flynn graduated as an architect from the University of Berkley. As a student, out of curiosity he became an affiliate marketer just to see if online marketing is a reality or not. In the year 2008, Pat Flynn started promoting products that he knew were genuine; when internet marketing was at its nascent stage. After graduation he got a job with an architectural firm and also found an amazing woman to marry. Life was indeed beautiful till he lost his job, just a couple of weeks before his marriage. But Pat didn't worry much as he had his affiliate marketing income to fall back on.

He started selling others products on Clickbank, Amazon, Commission Junction and a few other affiliate sites. Since it's free to become an affiliate marketer all he needed was a landing page for each product. Since he already had a blog www.smartpassiveincome.com he also promoted the products through his blog. Every time there was a sale, Pat approached Amazon to get the buyers details. Amazon gave him the email address of the buyer and that's how Pat built an email marketing list.

Then he started creating his own websites. Some of the businesses he created are www.foodtrucker.com , www.securityguardtrainingHQ.com , www.GreenExamAcademy.com to name a few. Food trucker is a site about meals on wheels. You can learn all you want to know on how to start a business in the food area where in you just hire a truck and use it as your kitchen. In Green Exam Academy Pat advised people about how to succeed in the LEED exam. Since he is an architect he knew about the importance of this exam. This drove traffic to his blog. The next blog talked about getting trained to become a security guard. These three blogs generated enough traffic for Pat to sell his products on them. Since Pat Flynn was genuine in giving tips that was helpful to people, he had repeat visitors. He started Podcast along with his blog and in six years time Pat reached a million downloads on his Podcast. He promoted them on social media and various forums. He invited people who had no skills to start their own business so that they can earn a living.

He had more than hundred affiliates selling his products online.

Pat charged $19.99 per download for his LEED exam tutorial that helped people to pass the exam. The tutorial was downloadable and once the payment was made the ebook got directly sent to the buyers email address. In the first month Pat made around $7000 and after that there was no turning back. How lady luck showered him with wealth was Pat put up his income online and made all his visitors take a look at it. Initially he was only earning through LEED course. Then he started foodtrucker and securityguardhiring blogs. He diverted the traffic that he got at the greenexamacademy page and since Pat had already established his genuinity visitors believed in him.

After two years Pat Flynn became a leader in the online marketing space with an income of more than $100,000 per month. Today his income is around $3 million per year.

Conclusion

Now that you've read the book, go ahead and become a super affiliate marketer. Open up accounts at various CPA sites and start promoting high value campaigns. Use all the tricks and tips mentioned here so that you can optimize your landing page, promote it on social media, get Google analytics installed on your site to hear the jingle of money. If Charles Ngo and others can make millions every year by being a super affiliate you can also become one. All you need is patience, time and unrelenting hard work. Keep at it and stay positive. Once you've mastered the art of CPA affiliate marketing then sky is the limit for your income. You too will start earning five figures thanks to CPA super affiliate campaigns. Go On! Identify ten programs that sell well and are contemporary and become a super affiliate in 2018. Live the big American dream of buying a swanky home, with two cars and lead the life you've dreamt till now in reality by being your own boss.

Tools

Remember in order to be successful in CPA Marketing

The tools you definitely need are:

Clickfunnels FREE 14 day trial copy and paste http://bit.ly/2qQYzKV

Auto responder Aweber Free 30 day trial>>> http://bit.ly/2D04WkZ

Any questions feel free to email me at krob817@yahoo.com

For one on one coaching contact me on skype live: official817

I ask you this question wouldn't you like to have enough money to quit your 9 to 5 job, take care of your family, and travel the world?

Yes

Then join

What others have been keeping a secret for so long.

Good Luck to your success!